CAKE
RECIPES

A teatime collection
compiled by Lucy Rose

Index

All-in-One Fruit Cake

A good, family fruit cake which is simplicity itself to make.

6 oz soft margarine	1 teaspoon ground mixed spice
6 oz granulated sugar	10 oz mixed dried fruit
2 eggs	2 oz glacé cherries, halved
2 oz self-raising flour	1 tablespoon milk
6 oz plain flour	Pinch of salt

Grated zest of 1 orange (optional)

Set oven to 325°F or Mark 3. Grease and base line a 2 lb loaf tin. Put all the ingredients into a bowl and mix until thoroughly blended. Put into the tin and bake for 1 to 1½ hours or until a skewer inserted comes out clean. Leave in the tin to cool.

Lemon Cake

A variation of a Luscious Lemon Cake which uses lemon curd. An all-in-one recipe.

5 oz self-raising flour	1 tablespoon lemon curd
1 teaspoon baking powder	Grated rind of ½ lemon
4 oz soft margarine	2 eggs
4 oz caster sugar	1 tablespoon water

Syrup:

Juice of ½ lemon	2 oz granulated sugar

Set oven to 325°F or Mark 3. Grease and base line a 2 lb loaf tin. Put all the ingredients together into a bowl and mix thoroughly with a wooden spoon for 3 minutes. Put into the tin and bake for 45 minutes or until a skewer inserted comes out clean. Meanwhile, for the syrup, mix the lemon juice with the sugar. On removing the cake from the oven, pierce the top all over with a fine skewer and, whilst hot, pour over the syrup. Leave in the tin to cool.

Coffee Butterscotch Cake

A coffee sponge with a buttery toffee flavoured filling and topping.

4 oz self-raising flour   **3 oz butter, softened**
4 oz caster sugar   **2 eggs, beaten**
1 tablespoon coffee essence

Icing:

2 oz butter   **5 tablespoons warm milk**
6 oz soft brown sugar   **6 oz icing sugar, sieved**
Glacé cherries or halved walnuts to decorate

Set oven to 400°F or Mark 5. Grease and base line two 6 to 7 inch sandwich tins. Sieve the flour and sugar together into a bowl. Cream the butter in another bowl, add the eggs, beat well together then mix in the coffee essence. Mix into the flour/sugar mixture and beat all together for one minute. Divide between the tins and bake for 25 minutes until golden brown and springy to the touch. Turn out on to a wire rack to cool. For the icing, melt the butter in a pan and stir in the brown sugar. Add the warm milk and simmer gently for 5 minutes. Cool a little, beat in the icing sugar and continue beating until thick enough to spread. Sandwich the cakes together with a layer of icing and cover the top with the remainder. Decorate with cherries or walnuts.

Frosted Walnut Cake

A delicious walnut sponge, sandwiched and coated with a scrumptious frosted icing.

4 oz butter, softened	**4 oz self-raising flour**
4 oz caster sugar	**Pinch of salt**
2 eggs, beaten	**4 oz chopped walnuts**

Frosting:

1 lb granulated sugar	**2 egg whites, whisked stiffly**
¼ pt cold water	**3–4 walnut halves to decorate**

Set oven to 350°F or Mark 4. Grease and base line two 6 to 7 inch sandwich tins. Cream together the butter and sugar in a bowl until light and fluffy. Beat in the eggs a little at a time. Fold in the flour, salt and chopped nuts and mix thoroughly. Divide the mixture between the tins and bake for 25 to 30 minutes until golden brown and springy to the touch. Turn out and cool on a wire rack. For the frosting, dissolve the sugar in the water in a pan and bring to the boil without stirring. Keep boiling until a little dropped into cold water forms a soft ball. Pour the syrup on to the whisked egg whites and beat hard until really thick. Quickly sandwich the cakes together with a thin layer of frosting and roughly coat the cake with the remainder, before the frosting starts to harden. Decorate with walnut halves.

Mincemeat Cake

This cake will keep well for several weeks.

4 oz butter, softened
4 oz soft brown sugar
3 large eggs, beaten

12 oz mincemeat
7 oz self-raising wholemeal flour
Milk to mix

Set oven to 325°F or Mark. Grease and line an 8 inch round cake tin. Cream together the butter and sugar in a bowl until light and fluffy. Beat in the eggs a little at a time then stir in the mincemeat. Fold in the flour and mix well, adding sufficient milk to make a dropping consistency. Put into the tin and bake for 10 minutes. Lower the oven to 300°F or Mark 2 and continue baking for 1¼ hours until the cake is firm, shrinking slightly and a skewer inserted comes out clean. Leave to cool in the tin for 15 minutes then turn out on to a wire rack.

Madeira Cake

A type of rich sponge cake, so called because in Victorian times it was served with a glass of Madeira wine.

4 oz butter, softened	**A few drops vanilla essence**
5 oz caster sugar	**8 oz self-raising flour**
2 eggs	**Milk to mix**
¼ teaspoon salt	**3 slices citron peel**

Set oven to 350°F or Mark 4. Grease a 6 inch round cake tin. Cream together the butter and sugar in a bowl until light and fluffy. Beat in the eggs, salt and vanilla essence a little at a time with a little flour towards the end. Fold in the remaining flour a little at a time with sufficient milk to produce a soft consistency. Put into the tin and bake for 50 minutes. Remove from the oven, arrange the slices of peel in the centre and return immediately for another 10 minutes or until a skewer inserted comes out clean. Allow to cool in the tin for 5 minutes then transfer to a wire rack.

Easter Cake

A type of Simnel cake. These cakes were originally baked for Mother's Day but are now more usually associated with Easter.

9 oz butter, softened
9 oz soft brown sugar
Grated rind of 1 lemon
5 large eggs, beaten
12 oz flour
½ teaspoon salt
¾ teaspoon ground mixed spice
¾ teaspoon ground cinnamon

6 oz raisins
4 oz sultanas
4 oz currants
3 oz glacé cherries, halved
3 oz chopped mixed peel
2 oz chopped almonds
Milk to mix
2 tablespoons apricot jam

10 oz almond paste

Set oven to 350°F or Mark 4. Grease and line a 9 inch cake tin. Cream together the butter and sugar in a bowl until light and fluffy. Add the lemon rind and beat in the eggs a little at a time. Sieve together the flour, salt and spices and fold in with the fruit and sufficient milk to produce a dropping consistency. Spoon half the mixture into the tin and spread out. Roll out half the almond paste to a 9 inch circle and place on the mixture in the tin. Spoon in the remaining mixture and make a hollow in the centre. Bake for 30 minutes, reduce oven to 325°F or Mark 3 and bake for a further 2¼ hours or until a skewer inserted comes out clean. Cool in the tin for 15 minutes then turn out on to a wire rack. Brush the centre and edge of the cake with jam. Roll out the remaining paste, cut into strips, plait and place on the jam. Decorate with coloured eggs.

Wholemeal Date and Ginger Cake

A good, family cut-and-come-again cake which keeps well.

6 oz butter, softened	8 fl oz milk
6 oz sugar	10 oz wholemeal flour
2 eggs	4 oz white flour
1 tablespoon golden syrup	3 oz chopped dates
½ teaspoon bicarbonate of soda	3 oz chopped ginger

Set oven to 350°F or Mark 4. Grease and line a 7 to 8 inch round cake tin. Cream together the butter and sugar in bowl until light and fluffy. Add the eggs and syrup a little at a time, beating well between each addition. Dissolve the bicarbonate of soda in the milk and fold in to the mixture, alternately with the flours, dates and ginger, mixing well. Put into the tin and bake for 1½ to 2 hours or until a skewer inserted comes out clean. Leave to cool in the tin for 30 minutes then turn out on to a wire rack.

Carrot and Walnut Cake

The grated carrot gives this cake a moist texture and the walnuts add crunch.

7 oz flour
2 teaspoons bicarbonate of soda
1 teaspoon cinnamon
Pinch of grated nutmeg
½ teaspoon salt

14 oz soft brown sugar
12 fl oz vegetable oil
4 large eggs, beaten
14 oz grated carrots
10 oz chopped walnuts

Frosting:

4 oz cream cheese
1½ oz butter, softened

4 oz caster sugar
3 drops vanilla essence

1 pineapple ring (tinned), chopped

Set oven to 350°F or Mark 4. Grease and line a 7 inch square cake tin. Sift together into a bowl the flour, bicarbonate of soda, cinnamon, nutmeg and salt. In another bowl, mix together the sugar and oil then mix in the eggs. Make a well in the flour, stir in the liquid then mix in the carrot and walnuts. Put into the tin and bake for 1 to 1¼ hours or until a skewer inserted comes out clean. Leave to cool in the tin for 5 minutes then turn out on to a wire rack. For the frosting, mash together the cheese, butter, sugar and essence then stir in the pineapple pieces. Spread thickly over the top of the cake.

Fudgy Chocolate Layer Cake

A superbly rich and toothsome chocolate cake.

3 oz plain chocolate, in pieces
7 fl oz milk
9 oz dark muscovado sugar
3 oz butter, softened

2 eggs, beaten
½ teaspoon vanilla essence
5 oz flour
1 oz cocoa powder

1 teaspoon bicarbonate of soda

Icing:
4 oz butter, softened
7 oz icing sugar

4 oz plain chocolate, melted
1 tablespoon milk
Grated chocolate to decorate

Set oven to 350°F or Mark 4. Grease and base line two 8 inch sandwich tins. Put the chocolate, milk and 3 oz of the sugar into a pan, heat gently to melt, then allow to cool. Cream the butter and remaining sugar in a bowl until light and fluffy. Gradually beat in the eggs, vanilla essence and milk mixture. Sift together the flour, cocoa powder and bicarbonate of soda and gently fold in, incorporating as much air as possible. Put into the tins and bake for 30 to 35 minutes. Turn out and cool. For the icing, melt the chocolate in a bowl over hot water and stir in the milk. Meantime, beat together the butter and sugar in a bowl then mix in the melted chocolate. Sandwich the cakes together with a layer of icing and coat the top and sides with the remainder. Decorate the top with grated chocolate.

Seed Cake

A type of Madeira cake flavoured with caraway seeds. This variation also contains almond essence rather than the more usual lemon flavour.

6 oz butter, softened	1 heaped teaspoon caraway seeds
6 oz sugar	8 oz self-raising flour
3 eggs, separated	3–4 drops of almond essence
	Milk to mix

Set oven to 350°F or Mark 4. Grease and line a 7 inch round cake tin. Cream together the butter and sugar in a bowl until light and fluffy. Whisk the egg whites in a bowl and then beat in the yolks. Combine gradually with the butter and sugar mix. Sprinkle in the caraway seeds and fold in the flour, adding the almond essence. If necessary, add sufficient milk to the mixture to make a thick batter. Put into the tin and sprinkle a few caraway seeds over the top of the cake. Bake for 1 hour or until a skewer inserted comes out clean. Leave to cool in the tin for 5 minutes then turn out on to a wire rack.

Genoa Cake

A popular light fruit cake.

6 oz butter, softened
6 oz caster sugar
4 eggs, beaten well
2 tablespoons single cream

12 oz flour
4 oz sultanas or currants
2 oz glacé cherries, quartered
Grated rind of 1 lemon

2 oz almonds, cut into shreds.

Set oven to 350°F or Mark 4. Grease and line a 7 inch round cake tin. Cream the butter and sugar together in a bowl until light and fluffy. Stir in the well beaten eggs and the cream alternately with the flour and beat very well. Add the dried fruit, cherries, lemon rind and almonds and mix thoroughly. Put into the tin, make a hollow in the centre and bake for about 1½ hours or until a skewer inserted comes out clean. Leave to cool in the tin.

Cherry Cake

This moist cake is well filled with glacé cherries

8 oz glacé cherries, halved
3 oz plain flour
3 oz self-raising flour
Pinch of salt
6 oz butter, softened

6 oz caster sugar
Grated rind of 1 lemon
3 eggs, beaten
3 oz ground almonds
Milk to mix

Set oven to 350°F or Mark 4. Grease and line a 7 inch round cake tin. Rinse the cherries, dry well on kitchen paper and toss in a little of the flour. Sieve together the flours and salt twice to mix thoroughly. Cream together the butter, sugar and lemon rind in a bowl until light and fluffy. Add the beaten egg a little at a time, beating well between each addition, keeping the mixture stiff and adding a little flour. Fold in the remaining flour, cherries and ground almonds with sufficient milk to make a fairly stiff dropping consistency; this will help to keep the cherries suspended evenly. Put into the tin and bake for 1 hour 20 minutes or until a skewer inserted comes out clean. Leave to cool in the tin for 5 minutes then turn out on to a wire rack.

Raisin and Orange Cake

This is a quick and simple all-in-one-cake. As an alternative, replace the marmalade and orange juice with 2 oz tinned apricots, chopped and 2 tablespoons of juice from the tin.

8 oz self-raising flour	**1 tablespoon orange marmalade**
½ teaspoon baking powder	**2 eggs**
4 oz soft margarine	**2 tablespoons orange juice**
4 oz caster sugar	**8 oz raisins**

Set oven to 325°F or Mark 3. Grease and base line a 2 lb loaf tin. Put all the ingredients together into a bowl and mix thoroughly for 2 to 3 minutes. Put into the tin and bake for 1½ hours or until a skewer inserted comes out clean. Leave to cool in the tin for 5 minutes then turn out on to a wire rack.

Saffron Cake

This is a simpler, no-yeast version of Cornish Saffron Cake.

¼ teaspoon saffron	12 oz self-raising flour
¼ pt milk	8 oz currants
4 oz butter	4 oz sultanas
3 oz brown sugar	2 oz chopped mixed peel

2 eggs, beaten

Put the saffron into the milk in a bowl and stand in a warm oven for 30 minutes to extract the flavour. Remove and set aside to cool. Set oven to 350°F or Mark 4. Grease and line an 8 inch round cake tin. Cream together the butter and sugar in a bowl until light and fluffy. Fold in the flour and then the currants, sultanas and candied peel. Beat in the eggs and the saffron milk and mix well. Put the mixture into the tin and bake for 1½ hours until golden brown and a skewer inserted comes out clean. Turn out on to a wire rack to cool.

Gingerbread

The recipes for gingerbread are legion and this one includes sultanas in the mixture.

4 oz butter	2 eggs, beaten
6 oz black treacle	8 oz flour
2 oz golden syrup	1 rounded teaspoon ground mixed spice
2 oz soft brown sugar	1 teaspoon bicarbonate of soda
¼ pt milk	2 teaspoons ground ginger
	4 oz sultanas

Set oven to 300°F or Mark 2. Grease and line a 7 inch square cake tin. In a saucepan, warm together the butter, treacle, syrup and sugar. Stir in the milk and allow to cool. Blend in the beaten eggs. Sift the dry ingredients into a mixing bowl, add the cooled sugar mixture and the sultanas and fold in gently. Put into the tin and bake for 1¼ to 1½ hours or until a skewer inserted comes out clean. Leave to cool in the tin for 5 minutes and turn out on to a wire rack.

Sherry and Almond Cake

This is a rich cake of good flavour which keeps well.

8 oz butter, softened   **7 oz self-raising flour**
8 oz caster sugar   **2 oz ground almonds**
4 eggs, beaten   **1 tablespoon sherry**
1 oz flaked almonds

Set oven to 350°F or Mark 4. Grease and line an 7 inch round cake tin. Cream together the butter and sugar in a bowl until light and fluffy. Beat in the eggs a little at a time. Fold in the flour and the ground almonds and, lastly, stir in the sherry. Mix all well together. Put into the tin, sprinkle the almonds over the top and bake for 2 hours or until a skewer inserted comes out clean. Leave to cool in the tin for 5 minutes then turn out on to a wire rack.

Honey Cake

Honey has traditionally been a popular sweetener, giving this cake a faintly gingery flavour.

8 fl oz clear honey	1 teaspoon bicarbonate of soda
3 oz butter	3 oz chopped mixed peel
12 oz flour	3 eggs
1 teaspoon baking powder	3 tablespoons milk
Pinch of salt	Grated rind of 1 lemon
1 teaspoon ground cinnamon	1 oz flaked almonds (optional)

3 tablespoons clear honey

Set oven to 325°F or Mark 3. Grease and line an 8 inch square cake tin. Put the 8 fl oz of honey with the butter in a saucepan and heat gently until melted, stirring continuously. Sift the flour, baking powder, salt, cinnamon and bicarbonate of soda into a bowl, then stir in the peel. Beat the eggs and milk together and stir into the honey mixture with the lemon rind. Make a well in the centre of the dry ingredients and add the honey mixture gradually, beating well between each addition. Put into the tin and sprinkle with the almonds, if desired. Bake for 1 to 1¼ hours until the cake is firm, yet springy to the touch. Using a fine skewer, prick the surface of the hot cake and pour on the 3 tablespoons of honey. Return to the oven immediately and bake for a further 10 minutes. Leave to cool in the tin.

Coffee Ginger Cake

A fat-less sponge with a rum, coffee and ginger filling and topped with coffee icing.

4 eggs	3 oz caster sugar	3 oz flour

Filling: 2 tablespoons rum
12 oz icing sugar
6 oz butter, softened
1 tablespoon coffee essence
2 oz crystallised ginger, chopped

Icing: 1 tablespoon coffee essence
6 oz icing sugar
2 oz chopped almonds for decoration

Set oven to 375°F or Mark 5. Grease and base line two 7 inch sandwich tins. Put the eggs and sugar into a bowl over a pan of hot water. Whisk until pale and creamy. Remove from the heat and fold in the flour a little at a time. Divide the mixture between the tins and bake for 20 to 25 minutes until golden brown and springy to the touch. Turn out and cool on a wire rack. Cut each cake in two lengthways. For the filling blend together the sugar, coffee essence and rum. Cream the butter until soft then gradually add the sugar mixture and beat well. Mix the chopped ginger with three-quarters of the filling to layer the cakes together and spread a thin layer, without ginger, around the side. Make a fairly thick glacé icing with the sugar, essence and a little water and cover the top of the cake. Press the almonds around the side of the cake and use the remaining filling to pipe rosettes around the top.

Marmalade Loaf

A tasty mix of ginger and orange flavours.

6 oz butter, softened
2 oz soft brown sugar
4 tablespoons golden syrup
2 eggs, beaten
5 oz ginger or orange marmalade

10 oz self-raising wholemeal flour
1 teaspoon baking powder
1 oz crystallised ginger, chopped
3–4 tablespoons orange juice
Marmalade and crystallised ginger to decorate

Set oven to 350°F or Mark 4. Grease and base line a 2 lb loaf tin. Cream together the butter, sugar and syrup in a bowl until pale. Gradually stir in the eggs and marmalade alternately with the flour, baking powder and chopped ginger. Mix in sufficient orange juice to make a soft dropping consistency. Put into the tin and bake for about 1 hour until golden and firm and a skewer inserted comes out clean. Turn out and cool on a wire rack. To decorate, melt 2 tablespoons of marmalade, cool slightly and spoon over the top. Decorate with slices of crystallised ginger.

Apple Cake

A spicy cake which contains glacé cherries and sultanas, the apple first being cooked to a pulp. This makes the cake very moist and hence a good 'keeper'.

3 cooking apples, peeled, cored and sliced
5 oz butter, softened
5 oz brown sugar
2 eggs, beaten
8 oz flour
½ teaspoon ground mixed spice

½ teaspoon ground cinnamon
½ teaspoon bicarbonate of soda
Pinch of salt
2 oz sultanas
2 oz glacé cherries, halved
Grated rind of half a lemon

1 dessertspoon Demerara sugar for sprinkling

Cook the apples with a little water until soft, then sieve to produce a smooth purée; there should be 4 to 5 oz. Allow to cool. Set oven to 350°F or Mark 4. Grease and line a 7 inch round cake tin. Cream together the butter and sugar in a bowl until light and fluffy, then beat in the eggs, a little at a time. Sift together the flour, spices, bicarbonate of soda and salt and stir into the mixture. Add the dried fruit. Mix the lemon rind with the apple purée and fold into the mixture. Put into the tin and smooth the top. Sprinkle a dessertspoon of Demerara sugar over the cake to give a crunchy topping. Bake for 45 minutes or until golden brown and springy to the touch. Cool in the tin for 15 minutes, then turn out on to a wire rack to cool.

Hazelnut Battenburg

A mocha coffee and nutty variation of this traditional favourite.

6 oz self-raising flour	2–3 drops vanilla essence
1 teaspoon baking powder	1 tablespoon cocoa powder
6 oz caster sugar	1 tablespoon strong black coffee
6 oz soft margarine	4 oz hazelnut chocolate spread
3 eggs, beaten	1 lb prepared marzipan

Caster sugar to decorate

Set oven to 375°F or Mark 5. Grease and base line two 1 lb loaf tins. Put the flour, baking powder, sugar, margarine and eggs into a bowl and beat well together. Spoon half the mixture into another bowl and beat in the vanilla essence. Add the cocoa powder and coffee to the remainder and beat again. Put one mixture into each of the tins and bake for 15 minutes until risen. Turn out and cool. Trim both cakes to make neat, matching rectangles then cut each in half lengthways. Sandwich one of each flavour together with chocolate spread and similarly join both pairs together, alternating, into a single block. Roll out the marzipan and cut large enough to wrap round the whole cake. Spread all four cake sides with chocolate spread, wrap around with marzipan, crimp the corners and trim the ends. Dust with caster sugar.

Boiled Fruit Cake

In this recipe, boiling the fruit makes it plump and juicy and therefore the finished cake is moist and flavoursome.

4 oz butter	**9 oz self-raising flour**
4 oz soft brown sugar	**1 teaspoon ground mixed spice**
8 oz mixed dried fruit	**1 egg, beaten**
¼ pt water	**¼ teaspoon salt**

Set oven to 325°F or Mark 3. Grease and line a 7 inch round cake tin. Put the butter, sugar, fruit and water into a saucepan, bring slowly to the boil and simmer for 5 minutes. Set aside to cool. Sift the flour and spice into a mixing bowl and mix in the cooled fruit mixture, together with the egg and salt, to make a thick batter. Put into the tin and bake for 1½ hours or until a skewer inserted comes out clean. Turn out on to a wire rack to cool.

Vinegar Cake

Being egg-less this farmhouse cake was usually made when the hens were off lay.
Thus it is suitable for those who do not or cannot eat eggs.

12 oz self-raising flour	8 oz Demerara sugar
4 oz butter or dripping	1 teaspoon ground mixed spice
8 oz mixed dried fruit	½ pt milk
2 oz chopped mixed peel	3 teaspoons vinegar

1 teaspoon bicarbonate of soda

Set oven to 350°F or Mark 4. Grease and line an 8 inch round cake tin. Sift the flour into a mixing bowl and rub in the fat until the mixture resembles breadcrumbs. Then add the rest of the dry ingredients except the bicarbonate of soda and mix well. Combine the milk and vinegar, stir in the bicarbonate of soda and then add the liquid to the dry mixture and mix well together. Put into the tin and bake for 1¾ to 2 hours or until a skewer inserted comes out clean. Leave to cool in the tin for 5 minutes, then turn out on to a wire rack.

Chocolate Coconut Cake

An unusual combination of chocolate and coconut flavours in a classic sponge mixture.

4 oz soft margarine	1 tablespoon cocoa powder
4 oz caster sugar	¼ level teaspoon baking powder
2 large eggs, beaten	1 oz desiccated coconut
4 oz self-raising flour	1 oz ground almonds

Milk to mix

Icing:	3–4 tablespoons hot, not boiling water
12 oz icing sugar	3 tablespoons cocoa powder

Set oven to 350°F or Mark 4. Grease and base line a deep 7 inch sandwich tin. Cream together the margarine and sugar in a bowl until light and fluffy. Beat in the eggs a little at a time. Sieve together the flour, cocoa and baking powders, add the coconut and almonds, fold in to the mixture and mix thoroughly. Add a little milk if necessary to make a dropping consistency. Put into the tin and bake for about 40 minutes until firm to the touch and a skewer inserted comes out clean. Turn out and cool on a wire rack. For the icing, sieve the icing sugar into a bowl. Dissolve the cocoa powder in the hot water, mix into the sugar and beat well. Use immediately, coating the top and sides of the cake and spreading evenly to a glossy surface with a knife warmed in hot water.

Victoria Sponge Sandwich

A quick and easy to make, all-in-one version of a teatime classic.

6 oz soft margarine	**1 rounded teaspoon baking powder**
6 oz caster sugar	**3 large eggs**
6 oz self-raising flour	**4 tablespoons raspberry jam**

Caster sugar for dusting

Set oven to 350°F or Mark 4. Grease and base line two 7 inch sandwich tins. Put all the ingredients, except the jam, into a bowl and beat well for 2 minutes until smooth and blended. Divide the mixture between the tins and bake for 25 minutes until golden brown and springy to the touch. Turn out on to a wire rack to cool. When cool, sandwich the cakes together with a generous layer of jam and dust the top with caster sugar. If desired, a layer of whipped cream can be added with the jam.

Rice Cake

As the mixture is very soft, do not use a loose bottom tin for this cake.

8 oz butter, softened	8 oz ground rice
8 oz caster sugar	4 oz flour
2 eggs, beaten	1 teaspoon baking powder
1 teacup hot water	

Set oven to 350°F or Mark 4. Grease and line a 7 inch round cake tin. Cream together the butter and sugar in a bowl until light and fluffy. Beat in the eggs a little at a time. Fold in the ground rice, flour and baking powder and mix well. Add the hot water and gently mix everything together. Put into the tin and bake for 1¼ to 1½ hours or until a skewer inserted comes out clean. Leave to cool in the tin for 5 minutes then turn out on to a wire rack.

Prune and Walnut Cake

Prunes make this richly flavoured cake moist and the walnuts give it a crunchy texture.

8 oz butter, softened	**1 oz cocoa powder**
8 oz soft brown sugar	**1 lb no-soak prunes, chopped**
5 large eggs, beaten	**6 oz chopped walnuts**
7 oz self-raising flour	**2 oz plain chocolate chips**

Set oven to 350°F or Mark 4. Grease and line an 8 inch square cake tin. Cream together the butter and sugar in a bowl until light and fluffy. Beat in the eggs a little at a time adding a little flour with each addition. Sift together the remaining flour and cocoa powder and fold in. Add the prunes, walnuts and chocolate chips and mix well together. The mixture should be of a soft dropping consistency. If too runny add a little flour or too solid add a little milk. Put into the tin and bake for 2 hours or until a skewer inserted comes out clean. Cover with greaseproof paper, not foil, if the cake is browning too quickly. Leave to cool in the tin for 30 minutes then turn out on to a wire rack.

Cider Cake

Soaking the dried fruit in cider gives a succulent flavour to this cake.

8 oz mixed dried fruit	**6 oz soft brown sugar**
4 tablespoons sweet cider	**3 eggs, beaten**
6 oz butter, softened	**8 oz self-raising flour**

1 teaspoon ground mixed spice (optional)

Put the dried fruit into a bowl with the cider and leave to soak overnight. Next day, set oven to 350°F or Mark 4. Grease and line a 7 inch square cake tin. Cream together the butter and sugar in a bowl until light and fluffy. Beat in the eggs a little at a time, then mix in the dried fruit and the cider. Fold in the flour and spice, if using, and mix thoroughly. Put into the tin and bake for 1 hour and 10 minutes or until a skewer inserted comes out clean. Leave to cool in the tin for 5 minutes then turn out on to a wire rack.

Sand Cake

A short textured cake made with cornflour and ground rice. A traditional teatime favourite or excellent eaten with a glass of fortified wine. The cake is best made with butter and the flavour improves if left for a day before cutting.

8 oz cornflour	**6 oz caster sugar**
1 oz ground rice	**2 eggs, large**
6 oz butter, softened	**Icing sugar for dusting**

Set oven to 350°F or Mark 4. Grease and line a 6 inch round cake tin. Sieve together the cornflour and ground rice. Cream the butter and sugar in a bowl until light and fluffy. Break in each egg separately, beating very well between each one, then carefully fold in the flour mixture. Put into the tin and bake for about 1 hour until light brown on top and a skewer inserted comes out clean. Leave to cool in the tin for 5 minutes then turn out on to a wire rack. When cold dust the top with icing sugar.

Orange Cake

An orange flavoured sponge with a luxury clotted cream and marmalade filling.

8 oz butter, softened	**1 heaped teaspoon baking powder**
6 oz caster sugar	**Zest and juice of 1½ large oranges**
3 eggs, beaten	**4 oz clotted cream**
10 oz flour	**3 tablespoons orange marmalade**

8 oz icing sugar

Set oven to 350°F or Mark 4. Grease and base line two 7 to 8 inch sandwich tins. Cream together the butter and sugar in a bowl until light and fluffy. Beat in the eggs a little at a time. Fold the flour into the mixture, add the baking powder, the orange zest and half the juice and mix well. Divide the mixture between the tins and bake for 25 to 30 minutes until golden brown and springy to the touch. Turn out and cool on a wire rack. Mix together the clotted cream and marmalade and sandwich the cakes together with this filling. For the icing, mix the icing sugar with the remaining orange juice and drizzle over the top of the cake.

Cherry Cobblestone Cake

*A beautifully rich and moist all-in-one cake, with plenty of cherries
in the mixture and on top.*

6 oz soft margarine	1 oz angelica, cut into small pieces
6 oz caster sugar	8 oz flour
3 eggs	½ teaspoon baking powder
4 oz sultanas	2 oz glacé cherries, halved
3 oz glacé cherries, quartered	2 heaped tablespoons apricot jam to glaze

Set oven to 325°F or Mark 3. Grease and base line a 2 lb loaf tin. Put all the
ingredients, except the halved cherries and jam into a bowl and beat until well
mixed, about 3 to 4 minutes. Put into the tin, smooth over and arrange the halved
cherries on top, in rows to resemble cobblestones. Bake for 2¼ to 2½ hours or
until a skewer inserted comes out clean. Leave in the tin for 15 minutes to cool
then turn out on to a wire rack. Glaze all over the top with boiled and sieved
apricot jam.

Sultana Cake

This moist cake keeps well and will improve in flavour if left for 48 hours before cutting.

8 oz sultanas	**Few drops of almond essence**
4 oz butter	**6 oz self-raising flour**
6 oz sugar	**Pinch of salt**
2 small eggs, beaten	**2 oz chopped nuts (optional)**

Put the sultanas in a bowl, cover with water and leave to soak overnight. Next day, set oven to 350°F or Mark 4. Grease and line a 6 to 7 inch round cake tin. Bring the sultanas and water to the boil in a pan then strain and mix the fruit whilst hot with the butter in a bowl. Mix in the sugar, eggs and almond essence. Fold in the flour and salt and mix well. Lastly add the chopped nuts, if desired, and mix well. Put into the tin and bake for 30 minutes. Lower the oven to 300°F or Mark 2 and continue baking for about a further 1 hour until firm in the centre and a skewer inserted comes out clean. Leave to cool in the tin for 15 minutes then turn out on to a wire rack.

Iced Coffee Sponge

A coffee flavoured sponge, filled and topped with coffee butter cream.

4 oz butter, softened	4 oz self-raising flour
4 oz caster sugar	Pinch of salt
2 eggs, beaten	1 teaspoon coffee essence

Filling and decoration:

4 oz butter, softened	3 teaspoons coffee essence
6–8 oz icing sugar, sieved	4 oz flaked almonds, toasted
A few chocolate drops (optional)	

Set oven to 350°F or Mark 4. Grease and base line two 6 to 7 inch sandwich tins. Cream together the butter and sugar in a bowl until light and fluffy. Beat in the eggs a little at a time. Fold in the flour, salt and coffee essence and mix thoroughly. Divide the mixture between the tins and bake for 25 to 30 minutes until springy to the touch. Turn out and cool on a wire rack. For the filling, beat the butter until soft and creamy and add the sifted icing sugar a little at a time together with the coffee essence. Sandwich the cakes together with a thin layer of filling, coat the side and top with the same and press the almonds evenly around the side. Make a pattern on the top with a fork and decorate with chocolate drops if desired.

METRIC CONVERSIONS

The weights, measures and oven temperatures used in the preceding recipes can be easily converted to their metric equivalents. The conversions listed below are only approximate, having been rounded up or down as may be appropriate.

Weights

Avoirdupois	Metric
1 oz.	just under 30 grams
4 oz. (¼ lb.)	app. 115 grams
8 oz. (½ lb.)	app. 230 grams
1 lb.	454 grams

Liquid Measures

Imperial	Metric
1 tablespoon (liquid only)	20 millilitres
1 fl. oz.	app. 30 millilitres
1 gill (¼ pt.)	app. 145 millilitres
½ pt.	app. 285 millilitres
1 pt.	app. 570 millilitres
1 qt.	app. 1.140 litres

Oven Temperatures

	°Fahrenheit	Gas Mark	°Celsius
Slow	300	2	150
	325	3	170
Moderate	350	4	180
	375	5	190
	400	6	200
Hot	425	7	220
	450	8	230
	475	9	240

Flour as specified in these recipes refers to plain flour unless otherwise described.